Stanmore College Learning Cen

00017163

D1765570

YORK NOTES

Books — be returned on or before

PYGMALION

GEORGE BERNARD SHAW

NOTES BY MARTIN WALKER

The Learning Centre
Stanmore College
Harrow HA7 4BQ
020 8420 7730

Longman

York Press

The right of Martin Walker to be identified as Author of this Work
has been asserted by her in accordance with the
Copyright, Designs and Patents Act 1988

YORK PRESS
322 Old Brompton Road, London SW5 9JH

PEARSON EDUCATION LIMITED
Edinburgh Gate, Harlow,
Essex CM20 2JE, United Kingdom
Associated companies, branches and representatives throughout the world

© Librairie du Liban *Publishers* 1997, 2003

All rights reserved. No part of this publication may be reproduced, stored
in a retrieval system, or transmitted in any form or by any means, electronic,
mechanical, photocopying, recording, or otherwise, without either the prior
written permission of the Publishers or a licence permitting restricted copying
in the United Kingdom issued by the Copyright Licensing Agency Ltd,
90 Tottenham Court Road, London W1T 4LP.

First published 1997
This new and fully revised edition first published 2003

10 9 8 7 6 5 4 3 2 1

ISBN 0-582-772702

Designed by Michelle Cannatella
Illustrations by Susan Scott
Typeset by Pantek Arts Ltd, Maidstone, Kent
Produced by Pearson Education North Asia Limited, Hong Kong

CONTENTS

The Learning Centre
Stanmore College
Harrow HA7 4BQ
Tel: 020 8420 7730

PREFACE

York Notes are designed to give you a broader perspective on works of literature studied at GCSE and equivalent levels. With examination requirements changing in the twenty-first century, we have made a number of significant changes to this new series. We continue to help students to reach their own interpretations of the text but York Notes now have important extra-value new features.

You will discover that York Notes are genuinely interactive. The new **Checkpoint** features make sure that you can test your knowledge and broaden your understanding. You will also be directed to excellent websites, books and films where you can follow up ideas for yourself.

The **Resources** section has been updated and an entirely new section has been devoted to how to improve your grade. Careful reading and application of the principles laid out in the Resources section guarantee improved performance.

The **Detailed summaries** include an easy-to-follow skeleton structure of the story-line, while the section on **Language and style** has been extended to offer an in-depth discussion of the writer's techniques.

The Contents page shows the structure of this study guide. However, there is no need to read from the beginning to the end as you would with a novel, play or poem. Use the Notes in the way that suits you. Our aim is to help you with your understanding of the work, not to dictate how you should learn.

Our authors are practising English teachers and examiners who have used their experience to offer a whole range of **Examiner's secrets** – useful hints to encourage exam success.

The General Editor of this series is John Polley, Senior GCSE Examiner and former Head of English at Harrow Way Community School, Andover.

The author of these Notes is Martin Walker, a writer, lecturer and English teacher. He has worked for many years at senior examiner level for a large English examination board.

The text used in these Notes is the Longman Literature edition, edited by Jacqueline Fisher (1991).

PART ONE

INTRODUCTION

HOW TO STUDY A PLAY

Though it may seem obvious, remember that a play is written to be performed before an audience. Ideally, you should see the play live on stage. A film or video recording is next best, though neither can capture the enjoyment of being in a theatre and realising that your reactions are part of the performance.

There are six aspects of a play:

1 THE PLOT: a play is a story whose events are carefully organised by the playwright in order to show how a situation can be worked out

2 THE CHARACTERS: these are the people who have to face this situation. Since they are human they can be good or bad, clever or stupid, likeable or detestable, etc. They may change too!

3 THE THEMES: these are the underlying messages of the play, e.g. jealousy can cause the worst of crimes; ambition can bring the mightiest low

4 THE SETTING: this concerns the time and place that the author has chosen for the play

5 THE LANGUAGE: the writer uses a certain style of expression to convey the characters and ideas

6 STAGING AND PERFORMANCE: the type of stage, the lighting, the sound effects, the costumes, the acting styles and delivery must all be decided

Work out the choices the dramatist has made in the first four areas, and consider how a director might balance these choices to create a live performance.

The purpose of these York Notes is to help you understand what the play is about and to enable you to make your own interpretation. Do not expect the study of a play to be neat and easy: plays are chosen for examination purposes, not written for them!

EXAMINER'S SECRET
A candidate who is capable of arriving at unusual, well-supported judgements *independently* is likely to receive the highest marks.

AUTHOR – LIFE AND WORKS

1856 Shaw born in Dublin

1876 Shaw goes to London

1879 Shaw takes a job with the Edison telephone company

1879–83 Shaw writes five novels – all of which are turned down by publishers

1884 Joins the Fabian Society

1888–90 Works as music, art and drama critic

1897 *The Devil's Disciple* staged in New York

1898 Marries Charlotte – an unusual and probably celibate marriage

1912 Shaw falls in love with Mrs Patrick Campbell but is afraid to follow it through

1914 *Pygmalion* first staged (in London) and is an instant success

1923 Shaw's career is revived by the Birmingham Repertory Company

1923 Writes *St Joan*

1929 Writes *The Apple Cart*

1929 The Malvern festival is entirely devoted to the work of Shaw

1938–45 Three of Shaw's plays are filmed – he retained complete script control

1950 Shaw dies (whilst pruning an apple tree)

CONTEXT

1856 Crimean War ends

1861–5 American Civil War

1874–80 Disraeli's second and last term as Primi Minister of Britain

1879 Zulu war with the British

1883 Edison invents the light bulb

1885 Karl Benz sells the first motor car and Marconi invent the wireless

1899–1902 Boer War is fought in South Africa

1900 Queen Victoria dies

1912 Alaska becomes part of the United States

1914–18 First World War

1920–33 Alcohol is prohibited in the United States

1922 Mussolini becomes prime minister of Italy

1924 Lenin dies

1929 The Wall Street Stock Market crashes

1933 Hitler appointed Chancellor of Germany

1939–45 Second World War

1950 Start of the Korean War

SETTING AND BACKGROUND

HISTORICAL BACKGROUND

By the end of the nineteenth century the landed gentry and the country agricultural labourer were in serious decline. Cheap imported food had reduced the importance of British agriculture. By 1911, the population of the United Kingdom had increased by 25 per cent in forty years, and over 75 per cent of that population were living in or near towns.

The first working-class MPs

After 1870 basic education was available to all and by the early twentieth century employers were faced with a literate and increasingly organised workforce. The lower classes could no longer be counted on to 'know their place'. Another sign of the decline of the landed gentry was the reduction of the powers of the House of Lords in 1911. However, members of Parliament in the elected House of Commons were given salaries for the first time. Working-class representatives could now afford to be MPs. Before this politics had generally been a rich man's preserve, often treated as a hobby rather than as a public service.

Strikes

The years 1911 and 1912 saw serious and violent industrial conflict. Soldiers were sent to deal with striking miners and railwaymen and several people were killed.

The suffragette movement

The suffragette movement was carrying out a vigorous and often violent campaign for votes for women. There were mass arrests after clashes with police. In June 1913, Emily Davison, a suffragette, was killed when she tried to stop the king's horse in the Epsom Derby.

However, there was some movement in attitudes towards women, who had few rights in law and who were often treated as property, especially in marriage. In November 1912, a Royal Commission on Divorce recommended that men and women should be treated equally by the divorce laws and it called for the grounds for divorce to include habitual drunkenness, cruelty and desertion.

EXAMINER'S SECRET

You will gain more credit if you show you have some understanding of the play in its historical context.

CHECK THE FILM

Shirley Valentine by Willy Russell is a film and a play in which an ordinary housewife escapes from the drudgery of her existence.

CHECK THE NET

Find out more about women's struggle to be given the vote. Enter 'suffragette movement' in any major internet search engine.

Poor medical care

There was still real deprivation and hardship in the country and, in 1913 Sir George Newman, the chief medical officer for schools, reported that more than half of the six million schoolchildren needed dental treatment, a third were unhygienically dirty and significant numbers suffered from tuberculosis, heart disease and skin complaints. Large families were common and many women died in childbirth.

The origins of the Labour party

The Fabian Society was an organisation which encouraged the development and exchange of ideas about social reform and industrial production. It aimed to bring better education, health care and increased prosperity to the majority and to break down class barriers, eventually creating a world community with justice and plenty for all. It was one of the groups which founded the Labour party. Shaw was a leading member and one of their most popular speakers.

THEATRE

Shaw the playwright

Shaw was always provocative and his plays were often concerned with uncomfortable issues. *Widowers' Houses* dealt with slum landlords and *Mrs Warren's Profession* with prostitution. 'My business …' said Shaw, 'is to chasten morals with ridicule'. He was not apologetic about teaching and preaching and in the Preface to *Pygmalion* he takes pride in being didactic, indeed he claims that great art can never be anything else.

At the beginning of the new century Shaw was the leading figure in the world of drama. He had gained great respect as a critic and he expounded the view that the dramatist should be primarily concerned with social issues and a new and challenging approach to morality.

Pygmalion

Shaw conceived the idea for *Pygmalion* in 1897; by the time it was first performed in London in 1914, he had become a successful critic, political writer and campaigner, showman and dramatist. He believed that there was a creative force within each of us struggling towards improvement and perfection (even in a poor flower girl).

DID YOU KNOW?

Visiting the theatre was a major pastime for the wealthy people of London. It was important to be seen at all of the fashionable places.

His own creative force was still active when he was ninety-four.

As a dramatist Shaw was not content to leave the staging of his plays to others. He took an active, often contentious part in directing. He was also a capable businessman. He suggested that plays should be put on in London for a limited season of six weeks and then tour the provinces before returning to London. He believed that this would extend the life of many plays and increase their profitability.

When *Pygmalion* was first performed in London it was a huge hit. This was especially welcome as Shaw had been going through a dull and unexciting period.

Shaw wanted the renowned Mrs Patrick Campbell to play the leading part. He had seen her play Ophelia in *Hamlet* seventeen years before and had conceived the idea then of her playing a cockney flower girl.

He did not dare offer her the part directly as he knew she would think it beneath her dignity so he invited her to a reading of the play and through a combination of trickery and flattery she was persuaded to take on the part of Eliza.

Shaw, always susceptible to women's charms, was swept off his feet by the great actress and, according to himself, 'was in love for nearly thirty-five hours'. Although he was sharp enough to prevent her taking over the running of the play, he wrote many love letters to his 'glorious white marble lady'.

Shaw had problems with both his leads. Mrs Patrick Campbell and Sir Herbert Beerbohm Tree, the actor-manager who played Higgins, were both very successful but set in their ways and they did not believe Shaw knew much about acting. Tree could only imagine a hero as being something like Romeo and Mrs Patrick Campbell upset Shaw by muttering her lines in rehearsals and moving the furniture around. Shaw eventually had the furniture screwed down.

However, *Pygmalion* was an enormous success wherever it appeared and whoever played in it.

CHECK THE FILM

Educating Rita by Willy Russell is a film and a play dealing with the education of a working-class woman and the changes that this brings about.

DID YOU KNOW?

Shaw believed that a group of international intellectuals (including himself of course) should run all world affairs.

In the late nineteenth and early twentieth century, many people involved in the theatre believed that drama should somehow reveal the truth about life, and show reality. Shaw felt that scientific study of humanity and society, the way people live and relate to each other, should be at the heart of theatrical drama. Like Strindberg (Swedish dramatist 1849–1912) and Ibsen (Norwegian dramatist 1828–1906), Shaw stressed the importance of thought and scientific method. Intelligence was more important than imagination. Reason should come before fancy. Tanner, a character in Shaw's play *Man and Superman*, says, 'the artist's work is to show us ourselves as we really are'. For artist we can read writer or dramatist.

DID YOU KNOW?

The play has four main themes which still make it relevant today:
- The role of women in society
- The importance of class background
- Education as a key to progress
- Different kinds of language

In England, some contemporaries of Shaw, like J.M. Barrie of *Peter Pan* fame, John Galsworthy, W. Somerset Maugham and James Bridie, wrote well-intentioned but dull dramas of ideas. Theatre audiences in London were generally upper middle class and women were in the majority.

In Ireland, the poet W.B. Yeats had helped found the Irish National Theatre Society in 1901 and together with the Abbey Theatre Company it produced an upsurge of realistic and romantic national drama, often very controversial and even provoking violent protest. Yeats wrote for the company and it also produced two dramatists whose work has survived the test of time: Sean O'Casey and J.M. Synge.

The popular taste in entertainment was for music hall variety shows with comic turns, acrobats and sentimental ballads. The first Royal Command Performance was held in December 1912 at the Palace Theatre before King George V and Queen Mary. On the bill were popular acts like Little Titch, Vesta Tilley and the Scottish comedian Harry Lauder who was a special favourite with the king. There was also a novelty ragtime band from America.

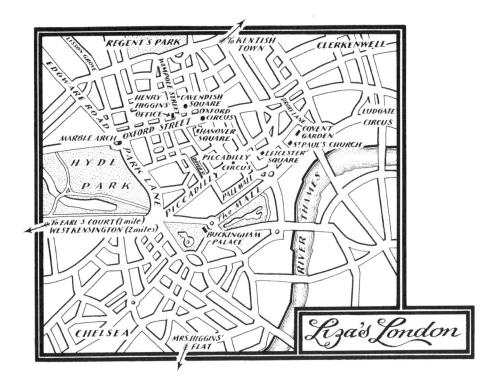

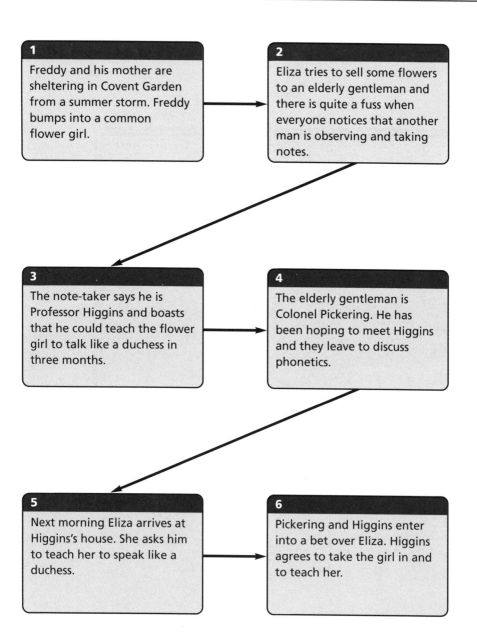

1
Freddy and his mother are sheltering in Covent Garden from a summer storm. Freddy bumps into a common flower girl.

2
Eliza tries to sell some flowers to an elderly gentleman and there is quite a fuss when everyone notices that another man is observing and taking notes.

3
The note-taker says he is Professor Higgins and boasts that he could teach the flower girl to talk like a duchess in three months.

4
The elderly gentleman is Colonel Pickering. He has been hoping to meet Higgins and they leave to discuss phonetics.

5
Next morning Eliza arrives at Higgins's house. She asks him to teach her to speak like a duchess.

6
Pickering and Higgins enter into a bet over Eliza. Higgins agrees to take the girl in and to teach her.

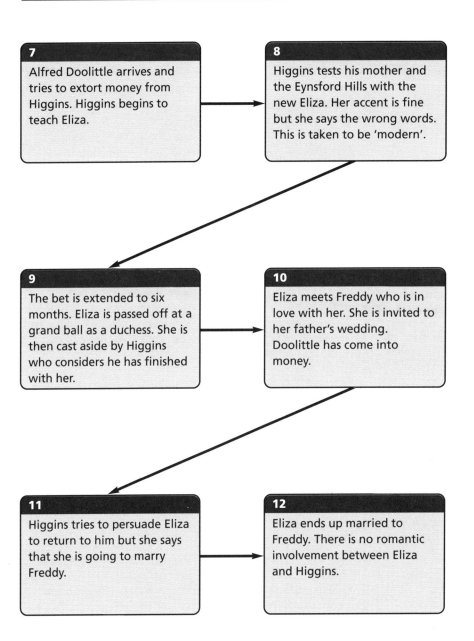

7
Alfred Doolittle arrives and tries to extort money from Higgins. Higgins begins to teach Eliza.

8
Higgins tests his mother and the Eynsford Hills with the new Eliza. Her accent is fine but she says the wrong words. This is taken to be 'modern'.

9
The bet is extended to six months. Eliza is passed off at a grand ball as a duchess. She is then cast aside by Higgins who considers he has finished with her.

10
Eliza meets Freddy who is in love with her. She is invited to her father's wedding. Doolittle has come into money.

11
Higgins tries to persuade Eliza to return to him but she says that she is going to marry Freddy.

12
Eliza ends up married to Freddy. There is no romantic involvement between Eliza and Higgins.

PART TWO

SUMMARIES

GENERAL SUMMARY

ACT I

On a summer evening, several people are sheltering from a heavy rainstorm under the front of a church in Covent Garden market. Freddy, an upper-middle-class young man, has been sent to find a cab to take his mother and sister home after a visit to a theatre. When he returns without one he is sent off again and bumps into a poor flower girl who calls him 'Freddy'. Freddy's mother wants to know how this common girl knows her son's name. She discovers that the girl calls all strange men 'Freddy' or 'Charlie'.

Eliza, the flower girl, tries to sell some flowers to an elderly military gentleman and one of the other people sheltering warns her to look out as someone is taking notes. This causes quite a fuss as Eliza is worried about being mistaken for a prostitute and protests loudly that she is a 'good girl'.

The note-taker is Professor Higgins, a phonetician, an expert in the study of the sounds people produce when they speak. He is taking notes as he has a great interest in dialects and accents. Higgins boasts that he could train Eliza to speak like a duchess in three months. The military gentleman, Colonel Pickering, is delighted to discover the man's identity as he has come to England to meet Professor Higgins. He too is an expert in dialects and specialises in Indian languages. Likewise, Higgins has been hoping to meet Pickering. They go off to have supper and discuss phonetics.

ACT II

Next morning, Eliza arrives at Higgins's house. She wants him to teach her to speak like a duchess so that she can get a job in a shop. Pickering is there and he bets that Higgins cannot do it. Higgins accepts the challenge and orders his housekeeper to scrub Eliza and to get her some new clothes.

Eliza's father, Alfred Doolittle, a dustman, arrives hoping to get money from Higgins in exchange for his daughter. He eventually settles for five pounds. Soon Higgins starts to teach Eliza.

CHECK THE FILM

This moment was famously captured in the film musical *My Fair Lady* (1964).

ACT III

After some time Higgins takes Eliza to his mother's house to see if she will pass for a lady among his mother's guests. The guests are the Eynsford Hills, the family who were waiting for a cab in the rain at the beginning of the play but they do not recognise Eliza as the poor flower girl. Freddy, the son, is fascinated by her. Eliza speaks with a very correct accent but she surprises the guests by her lurid description of her aunt's death. Afterwards, Mrs Higgins points out that Eliza is not yet ready for high society and that Henry may have created a problem. What about Eliza's future?

ACT IV

Before the period of the bet (now extended to six months) is over, Eliza has been a great success at an embassy ball. Back at Higgins's house, the two men are celebrating 'their' success, forgetting Eliza's part altogether and they are shocked and bewildered when she is angry with them. She is worried about her future and feels she has served her purpose and will be cast off.

Eliza leaves the house and meets Freddy Eynsford Hill who is in love with her and has been hanging around outside. They kiss and then wander the streets before getting a taxi to Wimbledon Common.

ACT V

Next morning, when Higgins discovers that Eliza is missing, he phones the police and goes to his mother's house. He is amazed when she tells him that Eliza is upstairs. Eliza's father arrives to invite Higgins to his wedding. He blames Higgins for making him respectable. Higgins had told a wealthy friend about Doolittle's interesting ideas about morality and the wealthy friend had left Doolittle a large sum of money.

When Eliza enters, Higgins tries to persuade her to return to his house, assuring her that he treats everyone the same. He says he misses her and suggests that he, Eliza and Pickering could live as equals. Eliza does not agree. She tells him that she is going to marry Freddy as soon as she can support him and goes to her father's wedding with Mrs Higgins.

AFTERWORD

To emphasise there was to be no romantic connection with Higgins, Shaw wrote an afterword which described Eliza's later life, married to Freddy.

DID YOU KNOW?

Many Victorians believed that the class system was vital to a stable society and that no one should attempt to change class.

DID YOU KNOW?

Eliza acquires a new accent whereas her father comes into money. Neither is really going to be accepted by the middle classes.

DETAILED SUMMARIES

PART ONE (pp. 7–10) – Sheltering from the rain

❶ The main characters are introduced.

❷ We hear Eliza's accent.

❸ Mrs Eynsford Hill reveals her snobbery.

A group of people of various sorts are sheltering from a heavy summer rainstorm under the portico of St Paul's church in Covent Garden. It is late evening and the theatres have just emptied.

Two ladies, Mrs Eynsford Hill and her daughter Clara are among the group. They are dressed in formal evening gowns as they have just come from the theatre and they are complaining about the length of time they have been waiting while Clara's brother, Freddy, has been searching for a cab to take them home.

When Freddy returns empty-handed they send him off to look again. As he rushes out he bumps into a poor flower girl who is coming in for shelter and damages some of her flowers. As she complains she calls him 'Freddy', which surprises Mrs Eynsford

CHECKPOINT 1

How is Mrs Eynsford Hill's reaction part of Shaw's **satire** on snobbery?

Hill who comments, 'Now tell me how you know that young gentleman's name' (p. 9).

Eliza, the flower girl speaks in a very strong cockney dialect when she asks Freddy's mother to pay for the damaged flowers. Shaw says that he will not try to represent the cockney dialect after this speech as it will be too difficult for most readers e.g. 'eed now bettern to spawl a pore gel's flahrzn...' (p. 9). He has left us with this example to demonstrate Eliza's dialect and to show what a difficult task Higgins sets himself.

Mrs Eynsford Hill pays for the flowers and asks Eliza how she knew her son's name. Eliza replies that she calls every strange man she meets either 'Freddy' or 'Charlie'.

PART TWO (pp. 10–19) – The note-taker

1 Higgins shows his skills with phonetics.

2 Pickering and Higgins meet.

3 The bet over Eliza is introduced.

It is raining harder than ever and an elderly gentleman who seems like a retired army officer takes shelter. Eliza asks him to buy some flowers and a man standing nearby warns her that someone is taking notes. Eliza begins to protest loudly that she is doing nothing wrong, 'I'm a respectable girl: so help me' (p. 10). She does not want to be taken for a beggar or a prostitute.

At first people think that the note-taker is a detective but then he puzzles them by imitating Eliza's speech and telling different members of the group exactly where they come from. The note-taker points out that the rain has stopped and people begin to go home. Mrs Eynsford Hill and her daughter go off to catch a motor bus.

The elderly gentleman and the note-taker discuss language and dialects while Eliza continues to complain and protest. Higgins behaves in an insensitive and offhand way towards Eliza. He takes no notice of her complaints and discusses her as if she were an object of scientific interest.

DID YOU KNOW?

This was one of the first times that a real accent had been portrayed on the page.

DID YOU KNOW?

Shaw invented his own form of phonetic language so that he could represent all of the sounds made in spoken English.

CHECKPOINT 2

What aspect of Higgins's professional conduct do we see here?

CHECKPOINT 3

How does Higgins reveal some of his arrogance here?

Higgins says his trick is 'Simply phonetics. The science of speech' (p. 15). Eliza begins to take notice of the men's conversation when she hears the note-taker boast 'Well, sir, in three months I could pass that girl off as a duchess at an ambassador's garden party' (p. 16). Eliza shows interest when Higgins boasts about his ability to do this and she follows this up in Act II.

The two men introduce themselves to each other. The note-taker is Henry Higgins, a professor of phonetics, the study of spoken language, and the elderly gentleman is Colonel Pickering, an expert in Indian dialects. This is a happy coincidence as they have both been keen to meet. They agree to go to Colonel Pickering's club to talk over supper.

CHECKPOINT 4

How does Eliza come across here?

Eliza makes a final attempt to sell Pickering some flowers and after a brief argument, Higgins throws a handful of money into her basket. She picks out the coins with loud exclamations of delight.

Freddy Eynsford Hill arrives with a taxi to find that he is too late. Freddy is a weak and ineffectual character, almost a fool. Eliza grandly takes the unwanted taxi off his hands and decides to go home in style. Eliza has ambition. She shows she has spirit and is able to stand up for herself. The taxi takes her to Angel Court, Drury Lane, an alleyway where she has lodgings, and the driver, admiring her spirit, refuses to take the fare.

Shaw's humour

The Act introduces us to the nature of Shaw's humour. Higgins addresses the sheltering people in a patronising and hectoring way. As Higgins shows off his brilliance we see Shaw's skill in exposing Higgins's insensitivity. The other characters in this scene are largely caricatures: the ineffectual Freddy, the whining Clara and the loud and raucous cockney flower girl. This is typical of Shaw's witty social commentary and he became well known for his humorous comments on manners.

Defining the different classes

In the opening Act we are given some idea of the differences between the classes – the elegant ladies and gentlemen in evening dress and the poor flower girl in her dirty and worn clothing. Freddy's mother is shocked that such a person should know her son's name. Shaw is outlining the clear differences so that the audience realises how far Eliza is from being a 'lady'.

The importance of language is introduced, a central theme of the play. Higgins believes that even the poorest girl may be passed off as a duchess if he trains her to speak in a certain way.

 CHECK THE WEB

Find out more about Shaw at the website **www.georgebernard shaw.com**.

GLOSSARY

phonetics the study of speech sounds

 Now take a break!

Who says?

1 'You really are very helpless, Freddy'

....

2 'How do you come to be up so far east? You were born in Lisson Grove'

....

4 'I came from India to meet you'

....

3 'I'm a respectable girl: so help me'

....

5 'What business have you at Bucknam Pellis'

....

6 'This an age of upstarts. Men begin in Kentish Town with £80 a year, and end in Park Lane with a hundred thousand'

....

About whom?

7 'Your mother's Epsom, unmistakeably'

....

8 'Yes, you squashed cabbage leaf … you incarnate insult to the English Language'

....

Check your answers on page 71.

PART ONE (pp. 20–32) – Higgins's laboratory

1 Higgins explains his trade to Colonel Pickering.

2 Eliza arrives wanting speech lessons.

3 Higgins and Pickering make the bet.

Next morning, Higgins is showing Colonel Pickering round his speech laboratory. The Colonel is very impressed.

Mrs Pearce, Higgins's housekeeper, enters and says there is a young woman asking to see him, 'She's quite a common girl, sir. Very common indeed' (p. 22) with a dreadful accent. Higgins sees this as an opportunity to demonstrate his recording machine and his phonetic writing systems to Pickering and he tells Mrs Pearce to bring the girl in. The young woman is Eliza. She has made some pathetic attempts to tidy herself and she has come in a taxi. When Higgins recognises her he is no longer interested. He has enough recordings of her particular accent and he tells her to be off.

Eliza protests at this treatment and announces that she has come to have speech lessons because she wants to get a job in a flower shop

EXAMINER'S SECRET

Keep a quotation book – select the key quotations and put them into a little book – this way you will get go know them far more easily than searching for them every time in a five-act play!

CHECKPOINT 5

What harsh aspect of Higgins's nature do we see here?

and she is ready to pay. She expects to be treated more politely when she says this, but Higgins continues in his usual bullying manner: 'Pickering: shall we ask this baggage to sit down, or shall we throw her out of the window?' (p. 23). In contrast, Colonel Pickering is very polite to her. When Eliza offers to pay a shilling an hour, Higgins realises that this is quite a large part of her income and he is impressed. He warns her that he would be a strict teacher. When Pickering challenges him to a bet Higgins accepts and claims he will be able to pass Eliza off as a duchess at the ambassador's garden party in six months' time – or even three.

CHECKPOINT 6

How does Pickering's treatment of Eliza differ from that of Higgins?

Higgins tells Mrs Pearce to take Eliza away and clean her and burn her clothes. Eliza does not understand his manner or his humour. He tells Mrs Pearce to keep her in the dustbin at one point. Eventually Pickering asks 'Does it occur to you, Higgins, that the girl has some feelings?' (p. 29), but Higgins takes no notice. He is only interested in the technical problems he has to deal with if he is to win his bet.

CHECKPOINT 7

In what way does Mrs Pearce show she is a sensible woman, if a little pessimistic?

Mrs Pearce's instincts tell her that no good will come of Higgins interfering in Eliza's life in this way. She is the only one to ask what will happen to Eliza when the experiment is over. Higgins just makes a joke of it. Mrs Pearce reluctantly takes charge of Eliza and leads her out to be bathed.

Contrasting characters

Higgins is obsessed with his work and has no time to be polite or considerate of people's feelings. He shows himself to be arrogant and intolerant.

Eliza shows that she has real ambition to better herself. Her efforts to improve her appearance and her offer of a shilling an hour for lessons are quite touching.

Mrs Pearce has serious doubts about the plan to teach Eliza to speak like a duchess. She thinks Higgins is careless where people are concerned and has not considered the girl's future. The housekeeper shows a good deal of sense when assessing the effects upon Eliza of Higgins's experiment.

PART TWO (pp. 32–49) – Eliza's bath, and Alfred Doolittle

❶ **Mrs Pearce makes Eliza take a bath.**

❷ **Pickering is a little worried about the intentions of Higgins.**

Mrs Pearce takes Eliza upstairs to bathe her. Eliza is very reluctant to have a bath and complains 'Ive never had a bath in my life: not what youd call a proper one' (p. 33). She has been in the habit of sleeping in her underclothes. However Mrs Pearce is very firm. She gets Eliza into the bath and scrubs her.

Meanwhile Colonel Pickering is questioning Higgins about his morals. He is concerned that Eliza should come to no harm while she is living in Higgins's house. Higgins reassures him that he is as unfeeling as a block of wood where female pupils are concerned. This is **ironic** as it is true but not in the sense that Higgins intends.

Mrs Pearce returns and asks if she may speak to Higgins. While expressing concern about Eliza's language and dress she gently asks Higgins not to swear in the girl's presence and to mend his table manners. Colonel Pickering is amused. After Mrs Pearce leaves, Higgins protests that he is much misunderstood. He is convinced that he is a shy, mild sort of person, but we, the onlookers, know that he is 'an arbitrary overbearing bossing kind of person' (p. 38).

PART THREE (pp. 38–50) – Alfred and Eliza Doolittle

❶ **Eliza's father tries to blackmail Higgins.**

❷ **Alfred Doolittle sees a changed Eliza.**

❸ **Eliza begins to like her new life.**

❹ **Eliza is quick to learn.**

Mrs Pearce returns to announce that there is a dustman at the door who has come about his daughter. Pickering is concerned but Higgins is confident he can deal with the man even though he says 'Of course he's a blackguard' (p. 38). Higgins is mainly interested in what sort of accent the dustman may have. Alfred Doolittle, Eliza's

> **CHECKPOINT 8**
>
> What does the bathing episode make the audience see about Eliza?

> **CHECKPOINT 9**
>
> In what way does Higgins lack understanding of people?

> **GLOSSARY**
>
> **blackguard** a villain

Part three continued

CHECKPOINT 10

What might the
audience admire
in Higgins's
behaviour here?

father enters. He is a bold man with an expressive voice. He
obviously hopes to profit from the situation and he demands his
daughter, expecting to be bought off. Higgins calls his bluff by
saying 'You dont suppose anyone else wants her do you?' (p. 39).
He then accuses Doolittle of plotting blackmail and extortion and
threatens to call the police. Doolittle backs down and tries to
explain his way out of this but Higgins is adamant and tells Mrs
Pearce to fetch Eliza.

CHECKPOINT 11

How does Shaw
make Alfred seem
comical in this
episode?

Eventually Doolittle says he will settle for £5. He entertains Higgins
and Pickering with his speech about being one of the 'undeserving
poor' (p. 43) who needs money just as much as the 'deserving poor'.
He makes no pretence that he will do anything but spend it on
pleasure and amusement. Higgins thinks he could make a good
politician or minister of religion out of him if he gave him speech
lessons but Doolittle will not hear of it.

 **DID YOU
KNOW?**

Only the wealthy
middle and upper
classes had access to
proper sanitation.
The poor lived in
filthy conditions.

He accepts £5 from Higgins and is on his way out when he meets
Eliza who is dressed in a Japanese kimono. He does not recognise
her and is amazed when she makes herself known to him. Higgins
and Pickering are also amazed by the change in Eliza's appearance.
Eliza has come to appreciate the washing facilities but was
embarrassed by the presence of a mirror in the bathroom. She
guesses the purpose of her father's visit: 'All he come here for was to
touch you for some money to get drunk on' (p. 47). Doolittle leaves
after advising Higgins to use the strap on Eliza if he wants to
improve her mind.

Eliza is pleased with the change so far and would like to show off to the other flower girls on Tottenham Court Road. She rushes off excitedly when Mrs Pearce says that her new clothes have arrived.

Later we are shown Eliza's first speech lesson. She is nervous and Higgins makes her more uncomfortable by striding around the room. Colonel Pickering is gentle with her and gives her encouragement but Higgins is rude and impatient, threatening Eliza with 'you shall be dragged round the room three times by the hair on your head' (p. 50). However he is pleased by her quick response to his instruction. He tells her to go and practise and Eliza leaves the room in tears. We are told that this is a sample of what Eliza is to suffer for months.

EXAMINER'S SECRET

Always have a spare pen!

Eliza starts to change

We are shown the tension between Eliza's wish to learn and Higgins's insensitivity and impatience tempered by Pickering's calming influence.

By the end of this Act, Eliza's appearance has been transformed and she has made the first steps in changing her speech.

DID YOU KNOW?

In contrast to the plot of *Pygmalion*, most Victorian plays were **melodramas**, based often upon real life crimes. Look at *Maria Marten* as a typical example.

Shaw draws humour from the observation of manners. The concept of a bathroom is totally alien to Eliza; a middle-class audience

Part three continued

would have found this amusing. Similarly, when she comes down to meet her father dressed in a silk kimono but does not feel dressed without her hat on, it is comic. The speech lessons bring humour to the play because:

- Higgins is interested only in the task in hand and in showing off his skill.

- Mrs Pearce is concerned for Eliza and there is humour in the diplomatic way in which she tries to suggest that Higgins's slovenly manners are not a good example.

- Pickering is concerned about Eliza's moral welfare.

- Higgins says that he is unfeeling where female pupils are concerned, which is true, but not in the way he suggests. He is in fact extremely insensitive.

EXAMINER'S SECRET

Plan your answers then you won't repeat yourself.

Now take a break!

WHO SAYS?

1 'you keep on listening, and presently you find they're all as different as A from B'

....

4 'Well, what would a man come for? Be human, Governor'

....

2 'shall we ask this baggage to sit down, or shall we throw her out of the window'

....

3 'Go home to your parents, girl; and tell them to take better care of you'

....

ABOUT WHOM?

5 'Have you ever met a man of good character where women are concerned'

....

8 'All he come here for was to touch you for some money to get drunk on'

....

6 'Have you no morals, man?'

....

7 'I rather draw the line at encouraging that sort of immorality'

....

Check your answers on page 71.

PART ONE (pp. 51–66) – Eliza's first outing

① Higgins takes Eliza to visit his mother.

② Eliza passes as a middle-class girl.

③ The other guests are tricked into speaking like Eliza.

Mrs Higgins, Henry's mother, is in her flat on the Chelsea Embankment. She is expecting visitors for an at-home day and is not pleased when Henry bursts in. She knows he always upsets her visitors with his odd manners and tactless remarks. She is rather surprised when he tells her he has invited a common flower girl to her tea party. She is not altogether reassured when Henry tells her he has taught the girl to pronounce words properly but 'She's to keep to two subjects: the weather and everybody's health' (p. 53). He tells his mother about the bet with Pickering.

Mrs Higgins's guests are shown in. They are Mrs Eynsford Hill and her daughter Clara, the ladies who were sheltering at Covent Garden at the beginning of the play. Higgins tries to leave but is too late and he is introduced to them. He is barely civil to the ladies and does not hide his impatience.

CHECKPOINT 12

What is clear about Higgins here?

Colonel Pickering arrives and then Freddy Eynsford Hill. Higgins recognises the Eynsford Hills' voices but cannot remember where he has met them.

Eliza is shown in and is introduced to the company. She is beautifully dressed and pronounces her words carefully and correctly. She makes a strong impression on the company. Mrs Eynsford Hill and her son suggest they have met Eliza somewhere before but it is obvious that they do not recognise her as the poor flower girl. Freddy is fascinated by her.

Eliza impresses the party by talking very precisely and knowledgeably about the weather, one of her prepared subjects. However she causes some surprise when she speaks about the strange circumstances of her aunt's death. Here she lapses into cockney slang such as, 'them as pinched it done her in' (p. 59) but Higgins covers up for her by telling the company it is the new fashionable way of speaking. He signals to Eliza that it is time she left and when she has gone he mischievously encourages Clara Eynsford Hill to use the new way of speaking when she visits other houses. Her mother is unsure about this and does not feel she can ever bring herself to use such language.

After the Eynsford Hills leave, Higgins asks his mother what she thinks about Eliza. Mrs Higgins says that Eliza looks fine but her conversation is not acceptable and is unlikely to improve in Henry's company. Pickering points out that Higgins's swearing has influenced Eliza and that 'I havnt heard such language as yours since we used to review the volunteers in Hyde Park' (p. 62). Mrs Higgins questions Henry and Pickering about Eliza's position in the house at Wimpole Street. They both chatter about how useful she is and what a brilliant student she has been. Mrs Higgins tries to point out that they have not thought about the problem of Eliza's future but they brush this aside and go off in good spirits. Mrs Higgins is exasperated.

CHECKPOINT 13

In what way does Shaw make Eliza's account of the weather seem humorous?

CHECKPOINT 14

What aspect of society life is Shaw poking fun at here?

CHECKPOINT 15

What does Mrs Higgins realise about Eliza's education?

> ### Shaw's humour
>
> Shaw creates a good deal of humour from observing very closely the ridiculous rules of 'polite' behaviour that existed in Victorian society. He shows the supposedly educated people to be extremely gullible.
>
> Humorous elements in this section include:
>
> - The Eynsford Hills' failure to recognise Eliza as the flower girl
>
> - Eliza's carefully pronounced but very technical comments on the weather
>
> - Eliza's lurid description of her aunt's death spoken in carefully pronounced upper-class tones but full of lower-class cockney expressions
>
> - Clara, so anxious to be in fashion, that she falls for Higgins's trick
>
> - Mrs Higgins treating her son like a naughty boy

DID YOU KNOW?

Swearing was severely frowned upon in polite society. Even the mildest swear words could cause extreme offence.

PART TWO (pp. 66–71) – The Embassy

❶ Eliza attends her first formal function.

❷ An old pupil of Higgins causes some confusion.

❸ Eliza is very well received and is declared to be a princess.

EXAMINER'S SECRET

Remember it is easier to learn in small doses than commit everything to memory at once.

Higgins and Pickering arrive at the Embassy party with Eliza. Eliza goes to the cloakroom and Higgins is accosted by an ex-pupil who claims to be an expert in European languages and who is attending the party as an interpreter. This adds another element of excitement to the experiment, though Nepommuck does not sound awfully convincing when he says things such as 'You are great cockney specialist' (p. 68).

The whole Embassy scene is full of pompous behaviour and wilful ignorance. Shaw's humour once again is aimed at the pretension of the middle and upper classes. Eliza is exhausted by her success. Everything seems like an **anti-climax** now. As in the story of 'The Emperor's New Clothes', the people would prefer, ironically, to believe the most fantastic version of events rather than believe that they have been fooled.

Eliza says she is not nervous as 'I have done this fifty times - hundreds of times ... in my day-dreams' (p. 68). She is presented to the ambassador and his wife as Pickering's adopted daughter. The ambassador is impressed and tells the interpreter to find out what he can about Eliza. The ambassador's wife questions Higgins about her but he pretends he does not know whom she is talking about. The interpreter returns and says that Eliza is a fraud but goes on to say that he believes Eliza to be a Hungarian princess. Higgins says that she is an ordinary London girl who has been taught to speak by an expert but no one will accept this. They prefer to believe she is a princess and Higgins is left on his own.

Pickering and Eliza join Higgins, and Eliza says she has had enough of being stared at and remarks 'I have done my best; but nothing can make me the same as these people' (p. 71). She thinks she has been unsuccessful but Pickering tells her that she has clearly won the bet for them. Higgins agrees that they should leave.

CHECKPOINT 16

How does Nepommuck's first assessment of Eliza make for a tense moment?

CHECKPOINT 17

What is Shaw saying about the upper classes here?

Part two continued

EXAMINER'S SECRET

Avoid topics that have nothing directly to do with the question.

The purpose of the Embassy scene

After Higgins has succeeded in his experiment and has won the bet, we are left wondering what happens next.

Shaw prepares us for Eliza's later reaction in the conversation between Pickering and Higgins. Higgins says 'Let us get out of this. I have had enough of chattering to these fools' (p. 71). Higgins's reference to Eliza as 'an ordinary London girl out of the gutter' (p. 71) reinforces our view of his insensitivity. This is bound to bring a reaction from Eliza eventually.

Now take a break!

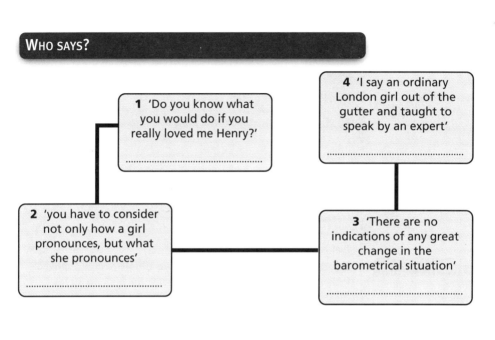

WHO SAYS?

1 'Do you know what you would do if you really loved me Henry?'

....

2 'you have to consider not only how a girl pronounces, but what she pronounces'

....

3 'There are no indications of any great change in the barometrical situation'

....

4 'I say an ordinary London girl out of the gutter and taught to speak by an expert'

....

ABOUT WHOM?

5 'We want two or three people. You'll do as well as anybody else'

....

6 'Do you mean that my language is improper?'

....

Check your answers on page 71.

PART ONE (pp. 72–80) – Eliza's anger

① Higgins has won the bet.

② Eliza becomes upset.

③ Higgins is more taken with Eliza that he wants to admit.

CHECKPOINT 18

Why is Eliza upset here?

CHECKPOINT 19

How does Higgins misjudge Eliza?

Higgins, Pickering and Eliza arrive back at the Wimpole Street laboratory at midnight. The two men make themselves comfortable and discuss the Embassy party. Eliza seems very tired. She is very quiet and obviously has something on her mind. When Higgins says 'Thank God it's over!' (p. 73) Eliza flinches.

Pickering has enjoyed the experience but Higgins says he has been bored by the experiment for some time. Eliza is visibly annoyed. Pickering goes off to bed after congratulating Higgins on his success. Higgins prepares to follow and gives some domestic instructions to Eliza.

When he has left, Eliza throws herself on the floor in a fit of rage and Higgins is shocked when he returns to look for his slippers and has them thrown at him. She says that now that she has won the bet for him '*I don't matter I suppose*' (p. 75). Higgins does not know how to deal with this situation and he tries to justify himself by demanding to know if she has been ill-treated by him or anyone else in the house. He suggests that she is suffering from nerves and exhaustion and he does not take her seriously when she says 'Where am I to go? What am I to do? Whats to become of me?' (p. 76).

Higgins has not given this much thought. He patronises her and says that as she is not bad looking she might find a husband to keep her. His mother may help her in this. Eliza rejects the prospect as little better than prostitution saying 'I sold flowers. I didnt sell myself' (p. 77).

CHECKPOINT 20

Why is Eliza appalled at the suggestion that she find a man and marry him for his money?

Humour and pathos

There is humour in the fact that Higgins and Pickering are unaware of Eliza's growing anger as Higgins dismisses her triumph as 'tomfoolery' (p. 73) and can only complain of how hard it has been for him. There is then comic stage business as Eliza throws her slippers at him. This is tinged with **pathos** as Eliza feels she has been cast aside now that she has served her purpose.

Higgins then says that Colonel Pickering may set her up in a flower shop as he has plenty of money. He will have to pay for her clothes anyway as he has lost the bet. Eliza wants to know if her clothes belong to her or Colonel Pickering and says 'I dont want to be accused of stealing' (p. 78). Higgins is hurt by this and is angered when Eliza insists that he take charge of her hired jewellery. She returns a ring he had given her and, in a temper, he throws it into the fireplace. Eliza feels some satisfaction when he tells her she has wounded him to the heart. He tries to leave the room with dignity but his temper gets the better of him and he slams the door. Eliza finds the ring but throws it back in the fireplace and goes upstairs in a rage.

CHECKPOINT 21

How does Shaw reveal the effect Higgins has on Eliza?

Higgins begins to suffer the consequences of his lack of forethought and his insensitivity to Eliza's worries. Here Higgins shows real emotion for the first time. He has always felt he was in control but his experiment has brought him unexpected complications.

PART TWO (pp. 80–2) – Eliza and Freddy

1. **Eliza meets Freddy and accepts his affections.**

2. **Eliza plans to ask Mrs Higgins for advice.**

Eliza changes into outdoor clothes and leaves the house. She meets Freddy Eynsford Hill in the street. He tells her he has been spending his nights there as it is the only place where he can feel happy. Eliza is touched by his affection and she responds to his kisses. They are moved on by a policeman. She tells him she was on her way to throw herself in the river. Such a dramatic death would have been in keeping with the popular entertainment of the day. Shaw is making a sarcastic reference to the plot of the typical Victorian melodrama.

CHECKPOINT 22

How does Eliza show she is developing according to her own free will?

DID YOU KNOW?

A young man and woman spending the night in each other's company might have been seen as scandalous.

Eliza and Freddy embrace again and are moved on by another policeman. Eventually they come across a taxi and Eliza suggests they drive around until morning.

Freddy has no money but Eliza says she will pay. In the morning she intends to 'call on old Mrs Higgins and ask her what I ought to do.' (p. 82). Although Eliza feels cast aside by Higgins she is ready to turn to his mother for help. Eliza is not ready to turn her back on Higgins completely.

Eliza is changing

Eliza has changed from a silly flower girl to a thoughtful young woman. Shaw deliberately makes Eliza seem more sensible and honourable than Higgins. Shaw is trying to make the audience see that people can not only imitate a better class but can better themselves through hard work.

Shaw was heavily involved with the early socialist movement in Britain and firmly believed that education could improve the lot of the ordinary man and woman.

Eliza is happy to find affection but she also shows independence and initiative. In contrast, Freddy is likeable but helpless.

 EXAMINER'S SECRET

Short, snappy quotations are always the best.

Now take a break!

WHO SAYS?

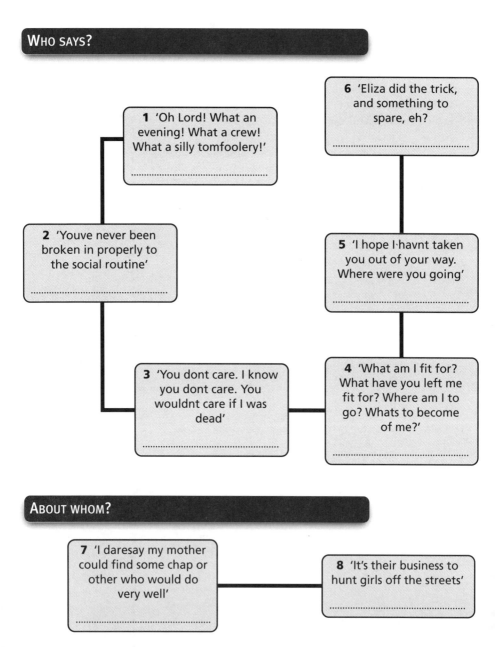

6 'Eliza did the trick, and something to spare, eh?

....

1 'Oh Lord! What an evening! What a crew! What a silly tomfoolery!'

....

2 'Youve never been broken in properly to the social routine'

....

5 'I hope I·havnt taken you out of your way. Where were you going'

....

3 'You dont care. I know you dont care. You wouldnt care if I was dead'

....

4 'What am I fit for? What have you left me fit for? Where am I to go? Whats to become of me?'

....

ABOUT WHOM?

7 'I daresay my mother could find some chap or other who would do very well'

....

8 'It's their business to hunt girls off the streets'

....

Check your answers on page 71.

PART ONE (pp. 83–97) – Looking for Eliza

① **Henry and Pickering look for Eliza.**

② **Alfred Doolittle has changed circumstances.**

③ **Eliza is in control of her life.**

④ **Alfred Doolittle feels forced to marry.**

Mrs Higgins is in her drawing room when her maid announces that Henry and Pickering have arrived and are phoning the police. She sends the maid upstairs to warn Eliza of their arrival and to ask her not to come down until sent for.

Higgins bursts in and tells his mother that 'Eliza's bolted' (p. 83). He is very disturbed. He makes excuses such as 'I cant find anything. I dont know what appointments Ive got' (p. 84). Mrs Higgins tells him that Eliza has every right to leave if she pleases. She is annoyed when she finds that Colonel Pickering has phoned the police and reported Eliza as missing.

> **CHECKPOINT 23**
>
> Why is Higgins so upset?

The maid announces the arrival of a Mr Doolittle, a gentleman. The two men cannot believe it is Eliza's father, the dustman, and guess that it is some respectable relative. However, it is Eliza's father but greatly changed. He is dressed in fine clothes as though on his way to a fashionable wedding. Doolittle complains bitterly to Higgins that he has 'Tied me up and delivered me into the hands of middle class morality' (p. 86). Higgins had jokingly recommended Doolittle as a moral philosopher to a wealthy American. The American had since died and left Doolittle £3,000 a year provided he gives lectures on Moral Reform.

> **CHECKPOINT 24**
>
> How does Doolittle bring humour to this scene?

This good fortune has complicated Doolittle's life. He is now expected to support his unemployed relatives and he will have to learn to speak middle-class English. Mrs Higgins suggests he could turn down the money but Doolittle confesses he does not have the courage to do this. He sees no future for himself as a poor man other than the workhouse and a pauper's grave. There is humour in the **irony** that Doolittle should find his good fortune such a burden. It is another example of Higgins's actions having unforeseen effects.

CHECKPOINT 25

What theme does Shaw revisit in this episode with Doolittle?

Mrs Higgins suggests that he will now be able to support Eliza but Henry objects, saying that he has paid Doolittle £5 for her. His mother tells him not to be absurd. She reveals that Eliza is upstairs but she makes Henry listen to her while she explains that Eliza was so angry and upset because once she had won the bet 'you two sat there and never said a word to her' (p. 90). She says that she herself would have thrown more than slippers at him. Colonel Pickering realises that they have been thoughtless in disregarding Eliza's part in the experiment, but Henry is not impressed and he sulks when his mother makes him promise to behave himself if she sends for Eliza. She asks Doolittle to go out on to the balcony until Eliza has made peace with Henry and Pickering and reminds Henry to behave himself.

CHECKPOINT 26

What is remarkable about Eliza's behaviour when she enters here?

When Eliza enters she behaves in a very calm and dignified way, addressing the two men formally and making polite conversation such as 'Quit chilly this morning, isnt it?' (p. 91). Higgins is annoyed and reminds her that he has taught all these tricks and has created her out of rubbish. He demands that she return home with him.

Colonel Pickering is uncomfortable and is made even more so when Eliza asks if he will wish to continue their friendship now that the experiment is over. She thanks Colonel Pickering for teaching her good manners. She says that this was quite difficult for her when Higgins set such a bad example with his temper and his swearing. She says that but for Colonel Pickering she would have been 'unable to control myself, and using bad language on the slightest provocation' (p. 92). Colonel Pickering taught her what it meant to be a lady by calling her Miss Doolittle from the first day at Wimpole Street and by his general behaviour and good manners towards her. Pickering is touched while Higgins sits grinding his teeth in anger. She makes her point by saying she would like Pickering to call her 'Eliza', and Higgins to call her 'Miss Doolittle'.

Higgins says he will see her damned first. Eliza refuses to be drawn into a row with him and says that leaving Wimpole Street is the final stage in her break with her former life. Pickering is upset that she is not going back. Higgins predicts that 'She will relapse into the gutter in three weeks without me at her elbow' (p. 94). She reassures Pickering that she could not go back to her old ways but Higgins is delighted when Eliza lets out one of her old yells at the sight of her father as he enters from the balcony.

> **CHECKPOINT 27**
>
> How does Eliza affect Higgins at this point?

Doolittle announces that he is on his way to church to be married to Eliza's stepmother, another result of joining the middle class. He asks Eliza to attend the wedding. She reluctantly agrees and goes off to get ready. Doolittle asks Pickering to go to the church with him to give him support. Mrs Higgins asks if she may go too and Doolittle says he would be honoured and she goes off to get ready, meeting Eliza on the way out and suggesting they travel together. Before he leaves with Doolittle, Colonel Pickering makes one more attempt to persuade Eliza to return to live at Wimpole Street.

 DID YOU KNOW?

Going to Doolittle's wedding shows that Mrs Higgins has accepted Eliza into her class.

PART TWO (pp. 97–105) – Eliza and Higgins

① Eliza tells Higgins what she thinks of him.

② Eliza is to marry Freddy.

When Eliza is left alone with Higgins she tries to avoid him but he confronts her and asks her if she is going to be reasonable now that she has had a bit of her own back. She says he only wants her to 'pick up your slippers and put up with your tempers and fetch and carry for you' (p. 97). Higgins says he does not intend to change and that he treats everyone exactly the same. Eliza tells him that she can bear to be treated badly but she cannot bear to be ignored or taken for granted. She says that he has no consideration for anyone.

CHECKPOINT 28

What side of Higgins does Eliza bring out?

CHECK THE BOOK

John Braine's *Room at the Top* (1957) is about the rise of an ambitious young man with working-class origins.

Higgins finally admits that he will miss her, that she has become an important part of his life. Eliza accuses him of trying to manipulate her and says she will not care for anyone who does not care for her. Higgins says this is like trading in affection and he rejects it. He admires her spirit and independence and tells her he does not want anyone slaving after him. She hits back saying, 'When you feel lonely without me, you can turn the machine on. It's got no feelings to hurt' (p. 99). He does not regret causing her problems as he believes that nothing would get done if we worried too much about making trouble. Eliza feels she has somehow lost her independence, her ability to earn her own living, by becoming a lady. Higgins suggests that he could adopt her or she could marry Pickering. She rejects both of these ideas and mentions that she could have Freddy for a husband and he at least loves her. Higgins tells her that she has a sentimental attitude and that she may as well go and marry a common man who will be sentimental with her and beat her when he is drunk.

Eliza is determined not to go back to Wimpole Street. She says she will get a job teaching phonetics and will marry Freddy as soon as she is able to support him. At first Higgins scoffs at both of these ideas. He thinks Freddy is foolish and useless. However Eliza makes him really angry when she says she might join with his Hungarian ex-pupil. He almost strikes her and she realises she has hit him on a sensitive spot, his professional reputation. Eventually he says he is proud of spirit and that now the three of them can live at Wimpole Street on equal terms. When Mrs Higgins arrives, Eliza tells Henry she will not be seeing him again. He tries to ignore this and to involve her in some details about shopping but she replies quite firmly and leaves with Mrs Higgins, as Henry tells his mother that she is going to marry Freddy and roars with laughter.

> **CHECKPOINT 29**
>
> How does Eliza outwit Higgins here?

Destroying stereotypes

Although Higgins admits he misses Eliza, he will not have anything to do with sentimentality. He wants a friendship of equals. Shaw did not want *Pygmalion* to be simply another obvious **romance**. It is difficult today to see the play as revolutionary but it does turn around some well accepted Victorian stereotypes such as:

- Eliza intends to support Freddy as she realises his upbringing has not prepared him for earning a living. This is a reversal of the expected roles of men and women.

- Eliza does not fall in love with the cold-hearted professor.

- Higgins does not become a completely changed man and see the error of his ways due to a love affair with Eliza.

EXAMINER'S SECRET

A feature of A-grade writing on literature is the ability to see two possibilities of interpretations and to support a preference for one of them.

Shaw takes the opportunity to comment further upon the inadequacies and pretensions of the middle classes, as represented by the Eynsford-Hills. Freddy, though inept, survives through Eliza's success but this would seem a disgrace to his mother.

AFTERWORD

Shaw wrote the afterword to dispel any ideas that Eliza and Higgins would eventually marry. He presents a series of events which includes Colonel Pickering helping Eliza and Freddy to open a flower shop. He had called the play a **romance** in the sense that it presented a series of unlikely events, not that it was a love story.

A romance?

It would be sheer sentimentality to suggest that Eliza would share her future with Higgins. Shaw's final comment is that 'Galatea never did quite like Pygmalion' (p. 118); similarly Eliza does not really like Higgins. Freddy and Pickering deserve Eliza's affection whereas Higgins does not.

My Fair Lady (1964) has a more conventional and romantic ending than *Pygmalion* – do you think Shaw would have approved?

Now take a break!

WHO SAYS?

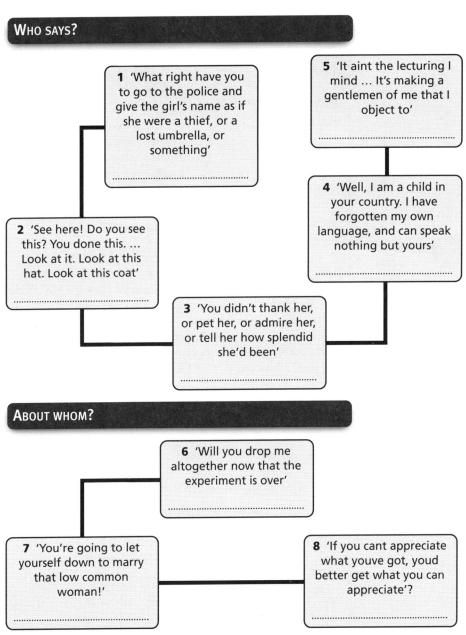

1 'What right have you to go to the police and give the girl's name as if she were a thief, or a lost umbrella, or something'

....

5 'It aint the lecturing I mind ... It's making a gentlemen of me that I object to'

....

4 'Well, I am a child in your country. I have forgotten my own language, and can speak nothing but yours'

....

2 'See here! Do you see this? You done this. ... Look at it. Look at this hat. Look at this coat'

....

3 'You didn't thank her, or pet her, or admire her, or tell her how splendid she'd been'

....

ABOUT WHOM?

6 'Will you drop me altogether now that the experiment is over'

....

7 'You're going to let yourself down to marry that low common woman!'

....

8 'If you cant appreciate what youve got, youd better get what you can appreciate'?

....

Check your answers on page 71.

PART THREE

COMMENTARY

THEMES

MOVING UP THE SOCIAL LADDER

The title *Pygmalion* is taken from a Greek legend, in which *Pygmalion* was the King of Cyprus. He fell in love with a statue that he had made and prayed to the goddess Aphrodite to give him a wife as beautiful as the statue. She did more than this, as she gave life to the statue. *Pygmalion* married the woman who was created; her name was Galatea. This Greek myth serves as a **metaphor** for the action in the play.

THE 'NATURE VERSUS NURTURE' DEBATE

The play reflects a debate that was taking place in society at the time. Famous writers such as George Bernard Shaw and H.G. Wells were part of a movement which felt that people could rise above the position into which they were born. Shaw explores this idea in *Pygmalion*. The debate is often referred to as *nature versus nurture*. This marked a major change in thinking from that of Victorian England. A basic belief of the Victorians was:

- A person is born into a class and so belongs there
- No one can move from one class to another

The new thinkers believed that:

- A person is not defined by the position into which s/he is born
- Through education, social change can be achieved

Since 1870 basic education had been available for all, for the first time. This led to people being less likely to 'know their place' and to old ideas being challenged. *Pygmalion* is part of that challenge.

THE SCIENCE OF LANGUAGE

There was great interest at the turn of the century in the idea of creating an alphabet which would allow English to be written down

CHECK THE BOOK

The Admirable Crichton is a play written by J.M. Barrie, and first performed in 1902. In it an upper-class household is shipwrecked and it is the butler, Crichton, who takes charge as he turns out to be the most capable person.

clearly, wherever in the country it was spoken. At the turn of the century there was neither television nor radio and so accents in different parts of the country were very strong. Shaw wanted an alphabet which could be universal and so make communication easier. At this time there was much interest among academics in the idea of making everything fit a pattern. This follows the thinking of the great Victorian scientist, Charles Darwin, whose *Theory of Evolution* allowed all living things on Earth to be classified. As part of this thinking, Shaw tried very hard to change the spelling system of the English language. He felt that a more scientific approach was needed and that the spelling system used (the one we still use today) was hopelessly confusing. He gave a famous demonstration of this by showing how the word *fish* could be spelt *ghoti* as follows:

DID YOU KNOW?
Shaw's play reflects the great interest in phonetics at this time.

- *gh* in *laugh* gives the sound *F*

- *o* in *women* gives the sound *I*

- *ti* in *nation* gives the sound *SH*

Shaw makes the invention of a phonetic system of writing one of the central ideas in *Pygmalion*. Henry Higgins is very successful because of his ability to reproduce any sound that is made in any accent. He does this through the use of an alphabet which has a symbol for every different sound that the human voice can make.

WOMEN'S SUFFRAGE

Shaw was a member of the Fabian Society and was involved in the Suffragette movement. This sought the vote for women and more acceptance of the equality of the sexes. He wrote many strongly worded letters on the subject and helped to raise public awareness of the Suffragette cause. When women protested about not having the right to vote they were arrested. They often went on hunger strike in prison and the authorities insisted that the women should be force-fed. A tube was pushed against her will into a woman's mouth or up her nose and liquid food poured down it. This killed many women and was denounced by Shaw as being totally inhumane. In a letter to *The Times* in 1913 Shaw wrote:

DID YOU KNOW?
Shaw denounced the brutal treatment of Suffragettes.

'I contend that this forcible feeding is illegal ... if the Government wants to break people's teeth with chisels, and force food into the lungs and run the risk of killing them, to inflict what is unquestionably torture on them, their business is to bring in a bill legalising these operations. They have no shame in doing it without the law. Why should they be ashamed of doing it with the law?'

Shaw's attitude to the equality of men and women is revealed through the way he has created the part of Eliza. Female characters in plays of the period were either old women or helpless girls who needed a man to rescue them. In *Pygmalion*, Shaw moves well away from this typical Victorian **melodrama** and makes Eliza a free-thinking character. Even though her speech changes, she does not become a mere reflection of Higgins but stands up for herself and wins her independence.

THE IDLE CLASS

When the play was first performed on the London stage in 1914, England was a very different country from the one it is today. Over three-quarters of the nation's wealth was owned by only one per cent of the population. There was a huge gulf between the rich and the poor and this gap was very difficult to bridge. The extremely wealthy upper classes owned most of the land in the country and made such a good living from their inherited money that they did not have to work. These people are **satirised** in the Embassy scene in Act III, where they are shown to be stupid and easily fooled.

The less prosperous middle classes looked up to their wealthier superiors and often attempted to copy their behaviour. The absurd speech of Freddy and Clara's readiness to adopt any new way of speaking that might be fashionable are examples of this.

EDUCATION FOR ALL

George Bernard Shaw believed strongly that everyone should have the right to an education. He felt that educating the population would bring about a better and fairer society. In *Pygmalion*, a simple flower girl is able to pass herself off as a duchess. Shaw felt that people should not be limited by birth, but should be given the opportunity to improve themselves. His aims for the Fabian Society were: 'to establish equality as the universal relation between citizens without distinction of sex, colour, occupation, age, talent, character, heredity or what not', and education was central to these aims.

EXAMINER'S SECRET

Try producing a single revision sheet for each of the key characters and themes. Set it out in the form or a diagram with essential quotations and some **phrases of your own**.

CHECK THE BOOK

Decline and Fall (1928) by Evelyn Waugh is a satirical attack upon the class system in England.

STRUCTURE

The play moves between four major locations as shown in the table overleaf. The scenes are mostly domestic and tension is developed through the interplay between Eliza, Higgins and Pickering.

Dramatic tension is also introduced and sustained through the experiment to pass Eliza off as a duchess. The pivotal moment of the play is the Embassy reception at the end of Act III (pp. 67–71). The first part of the play leads up to this moment with the question of Eliza's passing herself off as a duchess. The audience is shown that there is a great deal of work to be done with Eliza before this is possible and Shaw uses the episode at Mrs Higgins's at-home day to remind us of just how far Eliza still has to go.

There is an **anti-climax** once the bet has been won, and this leads to the drama of the emotional issues between Higgins and Eliza. This is unconventional on the part of Shaw. The audience of the day might well have expected that once Eliza had convinced people she was a duchess, there would be a romantic link between herself and Higgins and that the play would end with the romance of a marriage between the two. Shaw makes sure that there is as much action after the Embassy scene as there was before it.

The two characters of Eliza and Higgins are used by Shaw to put forward his views on his favourite subjects:

- The emancipation of women
- The breaking down of class barriers through education
- The development of a universal alphabet

The play is designed as an entertainment (remember that Shaw made money from *Pygmalion*) but also as a vehicle for some of Shaw's own ideas on society.

EXAMINER'S SECRET
There is not need to always provide lengthy quotations. Key words like 'tomfoolery' taken from the text can be more effective.

	Covent Garden	Wimpole Street	Mrs Higgins's flat	The Embassy	In the street
ACT I	Higgins and Pickering meet	Eliza – a poor and dirty flower girl	Eynsford Hill Family		
ACT II	Higgins and Pickering make a bet	Eliza bathed and changed – lessons begin	Mrs Pearce not in favour of the plan	Alfred Doolittle tries his luck	
ACT III	Higgins shows off Eliza	Eliza not quite ready	Ladies impressed by Eliza – Freddy in love	Mrs Higgins worried about Eliza	
	Higgins wins his bet	Eliza a success			
ACT IV	Higgins surprised by Eliza's anger	Eliza angry – feels useless and discarded			
	Eliza runs off with Freddy	Freddy waiting in the street to see Eliza			
ACT V	Higgins fails to persuade Eliza to return	Eliza to set up on her own and marry Freddy	Doolittle now rich – his wedding day	Mrs Higgins has taken Eliza in	

SIX MONTHS

CHARACTERS

HENRY HIGGINS

Henry Higgins is an intelligent, single-minded man. He is an expert in the field of phonetics, but he has allowed his work to become an obsession. Higgins is an example of a middle-class eccentric. He shows little sensitivity towards the feelings of others and many people, including his own mother, find him rude. Higgins likes to be the centre of attention and is a show-off. His desire to impress an audience sometimes leads him to behave quite tactlessly and his determination to succeed makes him seem ill-mannered.

Though Higgins does treat people badly, he does not intend to cause offence. He tries to explain this to Eliza in Act V, but his notion of treating everyone the same on all occasions does not excuse his bad behaviour. He is simply not very good at relating to people on a personal level and appears truly confident only when talking about his pet subject.

He is proud of his reputation and jealous of anyone who might prove better than him. This partly explains how annoyed he is when he hears that Eliza is to set herself up as a teacher of phonetics. He threatens to wring her neck when she says that she will teach his methods to the Hungarian. He is proud of having created the new Eliza and states that his work is more important than any one person.

Higgins does not feel that he has to behave according to anyone else's rules and his own views on life seem quite cold and impersonal. He bullies those who do not see things so clearly as he does and is actually quite proud of his lack of sentimentality.

Higgins is said to have been based on a real-life phonetics scholar, Henry Sweet.

Talented
Confident
Attention-seeking
Single-minded
Tactless

CHECKPOINT 30

How does Higgins view most people he meets?

 EXAMINER'S SECRET

It is always a good idea to collect a range of words and quotations to describe a character.

Quick-witted
Ignorant
Moral
Elegant

? DID YOU KNOW?

Eliza was a very unusual character because she was not dependent upon a man.

ELIZA DOOLITTLE

At the start of the play Eliza is naïve, simple and ignorant. She has grown up in poverty and has had to fend for herself. This has made her independent and able to look after herself. Despite her rough upbringing she has a strong sense of morality. She values her good name and is appalled at being thought of as a 'bad girl'. Unlike many girls in her situation, she has avoided the traps of crime and prostitution.

Eliza is ambitious to improve herself and is willing to grasp the first decent opportunity that arises. She is sensitive, as she shows in Act I (the Covent Garden scene) where she takes offence at the suggestion that she is behaving improperly.

As soon as she is presented with an opportunity, Eliza proves that she is quick to learn. She rapidly becomes a proficient student and the speed with which she learns astonishes even the cynical Higgins. Although she shows great strength of character and initiative, she remains vulnerable. We see this in her reactions to the insensitivity of Higgins's treatment.

Her need for affection leads her to respond to Freddy. He is an unlikely match for her and in fact she is going to have to look after him. In the final scene her grace and dignity show themselves clearly.

ALFRED DOOLITTLE

Doolittle is seen a loveable rogue. His upside-down morality is a source of amusement to the gentlemen, especially Higgins. He is amoral and quite shameless in his attempt at blackmail. He is happy in his station in life, even though he has to 'touch' (p. 47) others for money. He does not want responsibility and is proud of being one of the undeserving poor. He insists on taking £5 rather than £10 as he feels that £10 is so much money that it could not be squandered.

Loveable rogue
Amoral
Shameless

It is **ironic** that his skill in begging for money and his eloquence
when putting forward his odd views should be the cause of him
coming into wealth. Once he is wealthy, he complains bitterly of his
new responsibilities. He gains a host of new relatives, all of whom
expect his financial support. He feels that he will have to learn to
speak in middle-class English.

**DID YOU
KNOW?**

Shaw is mocking the
respectable classes
here for the way in
which they preached
to the poor.

COLONEL PICKERING

Pickering is an old-fashioned gentleman and scholar who has a
military background. He has spent many years in India and is an
expert in languages. He behaves like a kind uncle towards Eliza and
she appreciates that he always treats her like a lady. However, he is
drawn in by Higgins's enthusiasm and cannot resist the excitement
of the bet.

He acts as a foil to Higgins's insensitive behaviour of others and
often attempts to restrain the professor. There is something of the
schoolboy in him and he is not always aware of the effects of the
experiment upon Eliza. On occasion he talks to Higgins about Eliza
as though she were not there when she is actually in the room.

Sensitive
Gentlemanly
Schoolboyish

MRS HIGGINS

Mrs Higgins is the mother of Henry. She is a cultured lady who has
surrounded herself with fine things. An intelligent woman, she is
well aware of her son's bad behaviour and shortcomings, and treats
him quite firmly. As his mother, she understands his habits and
rash ways.

Mrs Higgins is concerned about what will happen to Eliza when the
experiment is over. She gives Eliza shelter when the girl runs away
from Higgins. She shows her generous and open-minded nature
when she:

- Entertains the Eynsford Hills, even though they are not
  fashionable

- Is prepared to attend Alfred's wedding

Although she is wealthy she does not behave snobbishly.

Cultured
Intelligent
Generous
Conscientious

MRS EYNSFORD HILL

A middle-class lady who has fallen on hard times. She does not have the money to keep up with polite society. She still behaves as though she is a member of Society and tries to develop friendships that may do her and her children some good.

CLARA

Clara Eynsford Hill is a snobbish, gullible girl. She is preoccupied with the latest fashions but shows that she has no judgement at all when it comes to deciding what is actually in fashion. She is easily fooled into thinking that Eliza's strange vocabulary is 'the new small talk' (p. 59).

FREDDY

Weak and
ineffectual

Freddy Eynsford Hill is a weak and ineffectual young man. He proves early on in Act I that he is not much use for anything when he is unable even to order a taxi. When one does arrive, he lets Eliza take it from him.

Higgins says that Freddy could not even get a job as an errand boy, even if he had the guts to try for it.

He falls in love with Eliza and provides much-needed affection for her. Eliza realises that she will have to support him as he was not brought up to work.

As Shaw comments in the Afterword: 'A clerkship at thirty shillings a week was beneath Freddy's dignity, and extremely distasteful to him besides' (p. 109). What Freddy really wanted was a job with a nice title and income, but entailing no work or effort. In Freddy, Shaw makes fun of upper middle-class affectations, with his 'Righto' and 'Ripping' (p. 82) slang.

 DID YOU KNOW?

Mrs Pearce is fairly typical of Victorian housekeepers in that she is sensible and dependable – rather like Mrs Hudson who looks after Sherlock Holmes.

MRS PEARCE

Like Mrs Higgins, Mrs Pearce is a sensible woman who treats people decently. She tries hard to cope with Higgins's behaviour, commenting tactfully on his bad language and poor table manners. She sees problems ahead for Eliza because of the experiment and is genuinely concerned for the girl.

LANGUAGE AND STYLE

The most obvious thing about the language used in the play is that it is all speech. We get to know about characters and situations from the words of those involved. This is of course true of all plays. What makes *Pygmalion* slightly more unusual is that it is a play all about language. Shaw wrote the play at a time when the way a person spoke said everything about that person. If you sounded well educated and likely to be from a wealthy background then you probably were. Likewise, if you sounded uncouth and rough then you were restricted to a particular place in society. In *Pygmalion*, Shaw explores the idea that changing the way Eliza sounds would be enough to convince people that she is something she is not.

George Bernard Shaw was a keen student of spoken language and clearly shows in the first words of Eliza that he is quite capable of portraying her cockney accent on the page. The thoughtful student will realise that although Shaw explained the need to abandon this early on, an actress portraying Eliza would still be talking with a pronounced London accent.

Shaw was very interested in the introduction of a phonetic alphabet which would have allowed all the sounds in spoken English to be written down without confusion. To illustrate this, Shaw set the play in London and chose to use the heavy accent of a cockney flower girl.

Though the play was intended for performance, Shaw always has an eye on the fact that it would also be read. The attempt in Act I to represent Eliza's accent in written form shows this. Shaw uses the idea that Eliza's speech cannot be written clearly whilst still retaining all its sounds, as an example of the inadequacy of our twenty-six-letter alphabet. Shaw developed a new alphabet which would allow all of the sounds used in spoken English to be represented accurately. Shaw attempted to simplify spelling by refusing to use apostrophies: e.g. 'dont', wont', 'youre'! Just think, no more spelling mistakes – ever. Needless to say, Shaw's big idea was not adopted.

EXAMINER'S SECRET

If you are asked to make a comparison, use comparing words such as 'on the other hand', 'however' and 'by contrast'.

DID YOU KNOW?

Shaw attempted to simplify spelling, refusing to use any apostrophes, e.g. 'dont', 'wont', 'youre'.

ACCENTS

The play features several accents:

EXAMINER'S SECRET

An A-grade student is able to provide a detailed account of language features, or structured patterns, to support a conclusion about the author's intentions.

- Eliza and Doolittle have broad London accents, using some words of dialect. For example:

  Doolittle: 'Bly me! it's Eliza!' (p. 46)

- Higgins, Pickering and Mrs Higgins use formal, standard English, with an emphasis on 'correct' pronunciation:

  Higgins: 'Yes, by George: it's the most absorbing experiment I ever tackled.' (p. 64)

- Freddy Eynsford Hill has a silly, pretentious, would-be upper-class accent, using phrases such as 'Ahdedo' (p. 55).

- Mrs Eynsford Hill and Clara are ready to use whatever new words or pronunciation may be thought to be fashionable. For example:

  Clara: 'Such bloody nonsense!' (p. 61).

Shaw also looks at the reaction to bad language. Higgins is supposedly a gentleman, yet he swears in front of Eliza, his mother and Mrs Eynsford Hill. Even the common Eliza does not do this, perhaps hinting that Shaw felt the middle classes to be hypocritical in the standards they applied to others. Higgins is ready to comment upon the speech of Doolittle and Eliza yet in may ways he is the worst culprit in the play with regard to swearing.

Above all, the play uses language to show that the way a person speaks cannot define the sort of person he/she is. The polite society of the time judged people by the way they spoke and Shaw shows this to be foolish. Shaw was very much against the idea that simply coming from a privileged background would mean that a person would receive a first-class education and go on to be successful in life. Freddy represents part of this idea. In terms of the sound of his voice, Freddy might be taken to be a well-educated young man, but Shaw makes Freddy's accent quite ridiculous.

Although the character who speaks with the most upper-class accent is the foolish Freddy; the two commonest speakers, Doolittle and Eliza, prove to be much more interesting characters altogether.

Mrs Eynsford Hill and Clara are made to seem foolish by Shaw. He makes them speak in a manner that might have seemed fashionable at the time. What Shaw is actually doing here is poking fun at the English middle classes who were always trying to make the right impression upon those higher up the social ladder. Clara's use of rather coarse language simply because she hears Eliza speak this way is intended to amuse the audience yet also to make some of them feel uncomfortable about their own use of fashionable slang.

Shaw's humour lies in the fact that though Eliza has learned to pronounce words correctly, her *choice* of words is often totally inappropriate, for example:

'They all thought she was dead; but my father he kept ladling gin down her throat til she came to so sudden that she bit the bowl off the spoon.' (p. 58)

When she is not making such mistakes as to discuss gruesome deaths in polite company, Eliza's speech swings too far the other way, for example: 'There are no indications of any great change in the barometrical situation' (p. 58).

Shaw is pointing out that it is not too difficult to change a person's accent but that it is another thing altogether to alter the whole way someone speaks. In the scene at Mrs Higgins's house, Eliza pronounces her words like a lady but still uses the vocabulary and sentence form of a cockney flower girl. The theatre audience are meant to pick up on this and to see what Shaw is doing with language.

Remember that points such as those above are not accidental. Shaw deliberately set out to ridicule the lazy and stupid well-to-do. The character of Freddy has been invented specifically to show this to the audience. Similarly, some of the supposedly 'common' characters have much more warmth about them than their better spoken middle-class counterparts.

EXAMINER'S SECRET
You will gain marks if you can make comparisons, such as between Higgins and Pickering.

EXAMINER'S SECRET

Shaw is in complete control of every word that his characters speak. If someone sounds odd it is because Shaw wanted this.

Alfred Doolittle uses the language of a common cockney but still manages to engage professor Higgins in argument. For all his apparent roughness, Doolittle is not put off by the greater learning of Higgins. Once he has come into money, Doolittle does not change his manner of speech. He could of course have had lessons in order to speak like someone with his wealth would have been expected to speak. The humour of the situation comes from the fact that he does not change his speech.

You need to be able to say sensible things about the writer's use of language. As you work through the play, select examples of your own which show how different characters speak. Be prepared to use these to support any comments you make about Shaw's choice of words.

Now take a break!

PART FOUR

RESOURCES

HOW TO USE QUOTATIONS

One of the secrets of success in writing essays is the way you use quotations. There are five basic principles:

1 Put inverted commas at the beginning and end of the quotation.

2 Write the quotation exactly as it appears in the original.

3 Do not use a quotation that repeats what you have just written.

4 Use the quotation so that it fits into your sentence.

5 Keep the quotation as short as possible.

When you use quotations in this way, you are demonstrating the ability to use text as evidence to support your ideas - not simply including words from the original to prove you have read it.

Your comment should not duplicate what is in the quotation. For example:

> Eliza asks whether her clothes belong to her or to Colonel Pickering, 'Do my clothes belong to me or to Colonel Pickering?' (p. 78).

Far more effective is to write:

> Eliza is confused and asks, 'Do my clothes belong to me or to Colonel Pickering?' (p. 78).

The most sophisticated way of using the writer's words is to embed them into your sentence:

> The fact that Higgins says, 'What does it matter what becomes of you?' (p. 75) in front of Eliza, indicates that he has a cruel sense of humour.

EXAMINER'S SECRET
In a typical examination you might use as many as eight quotations.

COURSEWORK ESSAY

Set aside an hour or so at the start of your work to plan what you have to do.

- List all the points you feel are needed to cover the task. Collect page references of information and quotations that will support what you have to say. A helpful tool is the highlighter pen: this saves painstaking copying and enables you to target precisely what you want to use.

- Focus on what you consider to be the main points of the essay. Try to sum up your argument in a single sentence, which could be the closing sentence of your essay. Depending on the essay title, it could be a statement about a character: Although Eliza has lived in poverty all her life, she has a clearly developed sense of right and wrong; an opinion about a setting: The use of Covent Garden Market allows all the characters to meet up, as it is one of the few places in which the different levels of society might have come across one another; or a judgement on a theme: I think that the main theme of *Pygmalion* is that no one is born to be anything. People are what their environment makes them: a duchess born into poverty would not behave like a duchess and a flower girl born into a wealthy family would not behave like a common street urchin.

- Make a short essay plan. Use the first paragraph to introduce the argument you wish to make. In the following paragraphs develop this argument with details, examples and other possible points of view. Sum up your argument in the last paragraph. Check you have answered the question.

- Write the essay, remembering all the time the central point you are making.

- On completion, go back over what you have written to eliminate careless errors and improve expression. Read it aloud to yourself, or, if you are feeling more confident, to a relative or friend.

If you can, try to type your essay, using a word processor. This will allow you to correct and improve your writing without spoiling its appearance.

EXAMINER'S SECRET

As you write, check that you are still answering the question. It is surprisingly easy to start well and drift off the subject entirely.

SITTING THE EXAMINATION

Examination papers are carefully designed to give you the opportunity to do your best. Follow these handy hints for exam success:

BEFORE YOU START

- Make sure you know the subject of the examination so that you are properly prepared and equipped.

- You need to be comfortable and free from distractions. Inform the invigilator if anything is off-putting, e.g. a shaky desk.

- Read the instructions, or rubric, on the front of the examination paper. You should know by now what you have to do but check to reassure yourself.

- Observe the time allocation – and follow it carefully. If they recommend 60 minutes for Question 1 and 30 minutes for Question 2, it is because Question 1 carries twice as many marks.

- Consider the mark allocation. You should write a longer response for 4 marks than for 2 marks.

WRITING YOUR RESPONSES

- Use the questions to structure your response, e.g. question: 'The endings of X's poems are always particularly significant. Explain their importance with reference to two poems.' The first part of your answer will describe the ending of the first poem; the second part will look at the ending of the second poem; the third part will be an explanation of the significance of the two endings.

- Write a brief draft outline of your response.

- A typical 30-minute examination essay is probably between 400 and 600 words in length.

- Keep your writing legible and easy to read, using paragraphs to show the structure of your answers.

- Spend a couple of minutes afterwards quickly checking for obvious errors.

EXAMINER'S SECRET

Always read the whole examination paper before you start writing.

EXAMINER'S SECRET

An A-grade candidate can analyse a variety of the writer's techniques.

EXAMINER'S SECRET

Always check your answer when you have finished.

WHEN YOU HAVE FINISHED

- Don't be downhearted – if you found the examination difficult, it is probably because you really worked at the questions. Let's face it, they are not meant to be easy!

- Don't pay too much attention to what your friends have to say about the paper. Everyone's experience is different and no two people ever give the same answers.

IMPROVE YOUR GRADE

Whatever text you are studying, it is vital that you are really familiar its contents. These Notes are intended to help you find your way around *Pygmalion* but they are not a substitute for reading and watching the play.

You need to develop a good knowledge of two major aspects of the play:

THE PLOT: Make sure that you know the order of events and how references early in the play affect events later on.

EXAMINER'S SECRET

A sign of a good candidate is the ability to cross-reference, e.g. provide evidence of Shaw's humour from different parts of the play.

THE CHARACTERS: Make sure you know who's who and what the various characters do and say.

Most students can immediately make some improvement in grade by recognising what it is that they are being asked to do. All written tasks can be broken down into the following simple areas:

- AIMS: what did the writer set out to do?

- MEANS: how did the writer go about doing it?

- SUCCESS: was the writer successful?

AIMS

You should consider the first point before you begin to write any lengthy answer. You must try to grasp what the writer has set out to do. In other words, was Shaw simply filling up three hours of stage time with *Pygmalion*? The plot could be summarised in a few pages, so why does the play take three hours on stage?

You might want to consider areas such as social comment. It is fairly obvious that Shaw was interested in raising issues such as the effects of the English class system. It might not mean too much to the modern student but such issues were of major interest at the time that the play was written.

EXAMINER'S SECRET

Examiners **never** take marks away.

There were many playwrights of Shaw's day whose work is no longer performed so perhaps Shaw was doing something a little different to his fellow writers. The plot of *Pygmalion* is quite complicated but it is the way that Shaw handles the various elements of plot that makes the play interesting.

Look at the way that one part of the plot is built up to the point where a major event is about to take place and then the scene shifts to another area of plot altogether. The audience is kept waiting on several occasions for the appearance of Eliza. Shaw develops tension by making us want to see whether she has changed from her last appearance.

EXAMINER'S SECRET

Higher-level achievement begins at the point when you show you are aware of being marked.

Remember: Shaw was a professional writer and he needed to please his audience.

Means

Many students concentrate on this second point only: how did the writer write the piece?

This results in a lengthy retelling of the story of whatever it is they have just read. There is nothing wrong with some account of the story but if this is all you do then you have carried out a fairly basic task. The plot of most great novels, plays and poems could be given to a class of eight-year-olds. They would then retell the story and draw a lovely picture. The skills shown by the eight year old students would not amount to much.

EXAMINER'S SECRET

Any marks gained by a lot of extra time spent on one question is unlikely to make up for marks lost on another.

Remember: simply retelling the story is not a high level skill.

Success

When you do come to discuss the way that the writer went about achieving his aims there are some basic things that you need to do.

- Decide what it is you want to say

- Select the parts of the text that support what you want to say (see **How to use quotations**)

All too often students make sweeping statements without backing them up. Try to make your comments precise and to keep them in focus with regard to the question you are answering. A question on the portrayal of class in *Pygmalion* does not require a discussion of every scene in the play. Good students know how to be selective.

To reach the highest level you need to consider whether the writer has been successful. If you think Shaw set out to create a believable character in Higgins, has he managed this? Do you think Shaw intended us to feel some sympathy for Doolittle and, if so, has he made us feel it?

EXAMINER'S SECRET

When writing about a specific scene or extract always make connections with the play as a whole – this at least shows you have read the complete work!

This area of your answer should reflect what you identified at the start regarding what the writer set out to do. If a horror film is not frightening then it is not successful: think in this way about the play. You need to consider whether *Pygmalion* works as a drama.

A higher-level answer will always contain the personal response of the student. Do not be afraid to say '**I feel that ...**' or '**I believe...**'. You must of course have some evidence for what you suggest. There are people who still think the Earth is flat but there is pretty good evidence that it is not.

Each time you make a major point you should support it, either by giving an account in your own words or by using a quotation.

Two major elements of language in *Pygmalion* – which tend to be seen by only the best students – are portrayal of accents and displays of wit.

You need to show that you know how the sound of speech can convey one thing but the content quite another. Doolittle is not formally educated yet speaks quite wisely on occasions, such as when he says his marriage is the result of 'Middle class morality' (p. 95).

Writers know these associations and play upon them for effect. Take the simplest idea of all – villain dressed in black; good person dressed in white. Such basic images occur throughout the history of world literature. Good writers do not simply use such basic images. They are constantly looking out for new things to use as comparisons. You need to recognise that this is how writers work and include references to it in your written answers.

Wit is a very big part of conversation in Shaw's plays. We would call wit 'intelligence'. Higgins clearly feels his wit is superior to that of Eliza but she ends up in a stronger position that Higgins in the end.

The final point to bear in mind is that your own writing needs to be of a high standard. You must attempt to use the language of literary criticism when discussing a work of literature. Simply saying **'the play was good'** does not really mean anything. It does not matter whether you liked the play; the important thing to remember is that you are commenting on the effectiveness of the work. Using vocabulary beyond that you might normally use when talking to your friends is vital if you wish to come across well on paper.

Don't forget the things you need to cover:

- AIMS: what did the writer set out to do?

- MEANS: how did the writer go about doing it?

- SUCCESS: was the writer successful?

Good luck with your writing about George Bernard Shaw and *Pygmalion*.

SAMPLE ESSAY PLAN

A typical essay question on *Pygmalion* is followed by a sample essay plan in note form. This does not present the only answer to the question, merely one answer. Do not be afraid to include your own ideas, and leave out some of those in the sample! Remember that quotations are essential to prove and illustrate the points you make.

What changes do we see in Eliza during the course of the play?

EXAMINER'S SECRET
Everything you write on your answer sheet is marked.

EXAMINER'S SECRET
If the rubric gives planning time, **use it** to plan your answers!

Look through the play for changes in her outward appearance (shown in stage directions), her manners and her language, and in others' reactions to her. You can either treat this theme by theme, or chronologically as shown here.

PART 1

- Refer to details from stage directions for Act I about her dirty, scruffy appearance, as a flower girl.

- She is loud with a very strong cockney dialect. Give example of her dialect e.g. 'Will yɔ-oo py me f'them?' (p. 9).

- She is almost begging in her manner as she presses the public to buy flowers, but she is confident and good at her job.

- Eliza defends her reputation and shows pride. She knows her rights and does not back down easily.

- She shows her ignorance when she thinks the man taking down notes is a policeman.

- Taking the cab home shows she would like a better life.

PART 2

- At Higgins's laboratory in Act II, she shows ambition, wants to better herself through speech lessons.

- Not stupid, she questions the intentions of the men. Quite aware that men might want to trick her; suspicious of the offer of a chocolate

- Ignorance shown when she sees the bathroom and thinks the bath is for boiling clothes

- Appearance changes dramatically once she is clean and wearing new clothes. Father doesn't recognise her

- Works hard and shows aptitude in the first lessons

PART 3

- At Mrs Higgins's flat, she has learned to pronounce and present herself well, but the content of her conversation is still lower class, e.g. discussion of her aunt's death.

EXAMINER'S SECRET

You are always given credit for writing your essay plans.

- Here we see that Eliza is intelligent enough to learn quickly but that she still has a great deal of catching up to do. In a matter of days she has learned to speak well enough to convince several people, even if most of them are rather stupid.

PART 4

- Her appearance at the Embassy is a great success, she has learned her lessons well.

- Eliza is mistaken for a princess but she does not overplay her part.

- Eliza has learned a little more restraint than she showed at Mrs Higgins's house.

PART 5

- Back at Wimpole Street wants to be valued as a person and not just part of a bet; still strong-willed, prepared to defend herself; shows pride

- Still vulnerable and concerned about her future

- Realises that being educated to be a lady does not fit her to earn a living

- Shows need for affection – Freddy

- Asserts her independence by leaving Wimpole Street

PART 6

- At Mrs Higgins's flat, shows dignity and restraint. Does not rise to Higgins's provocation

- Neatly plays off Pickering against Higgins – shows sophistication

- Realises how much she has changed but that she is still not accepted as a lady. Stands up to the bullying of Higgins and so impresses him

- Decides to marry Freddy and look after him – a reversal of the male/female roles

EXAMINER'S SECRET

Spend most time on the questions that offer most marks.

EXAMINER'S SECRET

Don't waste time looking at how your friends are doing!

EXAMINER'S SECRET

The answer booklet contains enough paper for you to get top marks!

CONCLUSION

- Changes in manners, language, appearance. But, unlike middle-class women, Eliza will still have to make her own way in life

- Her original ambition, self-reliance and energy will enable her to do this.

- She has come a long way from the common flower girl but still retains the honesty and sensitivity which made her appealing in the first place.

FURTHER QUESTIONS

EXAMINER'S SECRET

Keep an eye on the clock so that you do not run out of time.

1 How does Shaw present class differences in the play? You should refer to three of the characters.

2 The women in *Pygmalion* seem more sensible than the men. Discuss this, bearing in mind that Shaw was a strong supporter of the Suffragette movement.

3 Compare the attitudes of

- Higgins

- Colonel Pickering

- Alfred Doolittle

towards Eliza.

4 Discuss the nature of the relationship between Higgins and Eliza.

5 Discuss the character of Alfred Doolittle. How significant is he to the play?

6 How important is language in the play?

7 Explain how Shaw satirises pretence and snobbery in society. Refer to examples in the play.

8 What are the qualities that we admire in the character of Eliza?

9 Do you feel that there is any possibility of romance between Eliza and Higgins? Give reasons for your answer.

10 Discuss the elements of humour within the play. Give examples and explain why and how they are effective.

alliteration a series of similar consonant sounds, usually at the beginning of words. Alliteration is a *figure of speech* used to enrich the sound of a piece of writing or to give stress to a particular point

anti-climax a point where the plot does not achieve the expected climax, but becomes dull and digressive.

irony saying one thing whilst you mean another. Ironic statements are often made by characters who do not realise the full impact of what has been said. It can be used to achieve humour or pathos.

melodrama a piece of work, often a play, which relies upon sensational happenings and simple good/evil characters. Melodrama became very popular in Victorian England and such melodramas featured wicked villains plotting to trap virtuous maidens. A hero usually came to her rescue at the end of the piece.

metaphor a parallel image giving deeper meaning to the original subject-matter

pathos a quality which invokes pity and sadness in the reader or listener. It was used a great deal in Victorian literature: writers such as Charles Dickens were very skilful in using it to control the emotions of the reader.

pun a play on words in which a word with more than one meaning is deliberately used, suually to create humour

romance a work featuring unrealistic characters and storylines. Romances often deal with deeds of bravery in the pursuit of love and feature knights, dragons etc. Shaw calls *Pygmalion* a romance, but only in the sense that it is far-fetched and unlikely to happen

satire the intentional use of humour to make a vice or folly appear ridiculous

CHECKPOINT HINTS/ANSWERS

CHECKPOINT 1 Mrs Eynsford Hill is shocked when the flower girl calls her son 'Freddy'.

CHECKPOINT 2 Higgins is very confident about his teaching skills.

CHECKPOINT 3 Higgins's boast will later prove to be a little flawed.

CHECKPOINT 4 Eliza is most undignified here, scrabbling for coins and making uncouth noises.

CHECKPOINT 5 Higgins is not interested in people unless they are useful to his work.

CHECKPOINT 6 Colonel Pickering is an old-fashioned gentleman who treats Eliza with politeness and kindness.

CHECKPOINT 7 Mrs Pearce foresees problems as she realises that Eliza will not be able to fit into polite society no matter how she speaks.

CHECKPOINT 8 Whilst amused by this we are reminded of Eliza's poverty and ignorance – she thinks bathing is harmful.

CHECKPOINT 9 Higgins has little understanding of the impression he makes on other people. he does not seem to realise just how rude he actually is.

CHECKPOINT 10 The way Higgins calls Doolittle's bluff.

CHECKPOINT 11 Doolittle explains his philosophy saying he cannot afford to have morals. His blunt honesty about his own scheming creates humour.

CHECKPOINT 12 Higgins is uncomfortable in polite society.

CHECKPOINT 13 Eliza speaks like a modern weather presenter using technical terms that would not form part of everyday conversation.

CHECKPOINT 14 The obsession with following new trends, no matter how silly they might be.

CHECKPOINT 15 Mrs Higgins foresees problems if Eliza is constantly exposed to the swearing of Higgins.

CHECKPOINT 16 He declares her to be a fraud – but not for the right reasons.

CHECKPOINT 17 Shaw is poking fun at upper-class gullibility.

CHECKPOINT 18 Higgins shows her no respect and seems ready to discard her now she is no longer part of his experiment.

CHECKPOINT 19 Higgins is unaware of Eliza's growing anger.

CHECKPOINT 20 Eliza has a keen sense of morality and will not sell herself.

CHECKPOINT 21 Higgins begins to suffer the consequences of his lack of forethought and his insensitivity to Eliza's worries.

CHECKPOINT 22 Eliza takes charge of the situation with Freddy.

CHECKPOINT 23 He pretends it is because he relies on Eliza as a kind of secretary. Really it is that she has acted on her own and also that he has become fond of her.

CHECKPOINT 24 Doolittle complains of his good fortune.

CHECKPOINT 25 The theme of false middle - class morals. Shaw uses Doolittle to highlight the obsessions with everything being 'proper'.

CHECKPOINT 26 Note how cool and dignified Eliza is.

CHECKPOINT 27 Eliza makes Higgins squirm by praising Colonel Pickering.

CHECKPOINT 28 Higgins admits he will miss Eliza. He claims not to be sentimental but has grown to rely upon her.

CHECKPOINT 29 Eliza finds Higgins's weak spot.

CHECKPOINT 30 He treats people as things upon which to experiment.

TEST YOURSELF (ACT I)

1 Mrs Eynsford Hill (The Mother)

2 Higgins (The Note Taker)

3 Eliza (The Flower Girl)

4 Pickering

5 The Taximan

6 Higgins

7 Mrs Eynsford Hill (The Mother)

8 Eliza (The Flower Girl)

TEST YOURSELF (ACT II)

1 Higgins

2 Higgins

3 Mrs Pearce

4 Alfred Doolittle

5 Pickering

6 Alfred Doolittle

7 Alfred Doolittle

8 Alfred Doolittle (he) and Higgins (you)

TEST YOURSELF (ACT III)

1 Mrs Higgins

2 Higgins

3 Eliza

4 Higgins

5 The Eynsford Hills

6 Mrs Higgins

TEST YOURSELF (ACT IV)

1 Higgins

2 Pickering

3 Eliza

4 Eliza

5 Freddy

6 Pickering

7 Eliza

8 The Police

TEST YOURSELF (ACT V)

1 Mrs Higgins

2 Alfred Doolittle

3 Mrs Higgins

4 Eliza

5 Alfred Doolittle

6 Pickering

7 Alfred Doolittle

8 Eliza

NOTES

NOTES

Maya Angelou
I Know Why the Caged Bird Sings

Jane Austen
Pride and Prejudice

Alan Ayckbourn
Absent Friends

Elizabeth Barrett Browning
Selected Poems

Robert Bolt
A Man for All Seasons

Harold Brighouse
Hobson's Choice

Charlotte Brontë
Jane Eyre

Emily Brontë
Wuthering Heights

Shelagh Delaney
A Taste of Honey

Charles Dickens
David Copperfield
Great Expectations
Hard Times
Oliver Twist

Roddy Doyle
Paddy Clarke Ha Ha Ha

George Eliot
Silas Marner
The Mill on the Floss

Anne Frank
The Diary of a Young Girl

William Golding
Lord of the Flies

Oliver Goldsmith
She Stoops to Conquer

Willis Hall
The Long and the Short and the Tall

Thomas Hardy
Far from the Madding Crowd

The Mayor of Casterbridge
Tess of the d'Urbervilles
The Withered Arm and other Wessex Tales

L.P. Hartley
The Go-Between

Seamus Heaney
Selected Poems

Susan Hill
I'm the King of the Castle

Barry Hines
A Kestrel for a Knave

Louise Lawrence
Children of the Dust

Harper Lee
To Kill a Mockingbird

Laurie Lee
Cider with Rosie

Arthur Miller
The Crucible
A View from the Bridge

Robert O'Brien
Z for Zachariah

Frank O'Connor
My Oedipus Complex and Other Stories

George Orwell
Animal Farm

J.B. Priestley
An Inspector Calls
When We Are Married

Willy Russell
Educating Rita
Our Day Out

J.D. Salinger
The Catcher in the Rye

William Shakespeare
Henry IV Part I
Henry V
Julius Caesar
Macbeth

The Merchant of Venice
A Midsummer Night's Dream
Much Ado About Nothing
Romeo and Juliet
The Tempest
Twelfth Night

George Bernard Shaw
Pygmalion

Mary Shelley
Frankenstein

R.C. Sherriff
Journey's End

Rukshana Smith
Salt on the snow

John Steinbeck
Of Mice and Men

Robert Louis Stevenson
Dr Jekyll and Mr Hyde

Jonathan Swift
Gulliver's Travels

Robert Swindells
Daz 4 Zoe

Mildred D. Taylor
Roll of Thunder, Hear My Cry

Mark Twain
Huckleberry Finn

James Watson
Talking in Whispers

Edith Wharton
Ethan Frome

William Wordsworth
Selected Poems

A Choice of Poets

Mystery Stories of the Nineteenth Century including The Signalman

Nineteenth Century Short Stories

Poetry of the First World War

Six Women Poets